# London City Sketch
# Adult Coloring Book

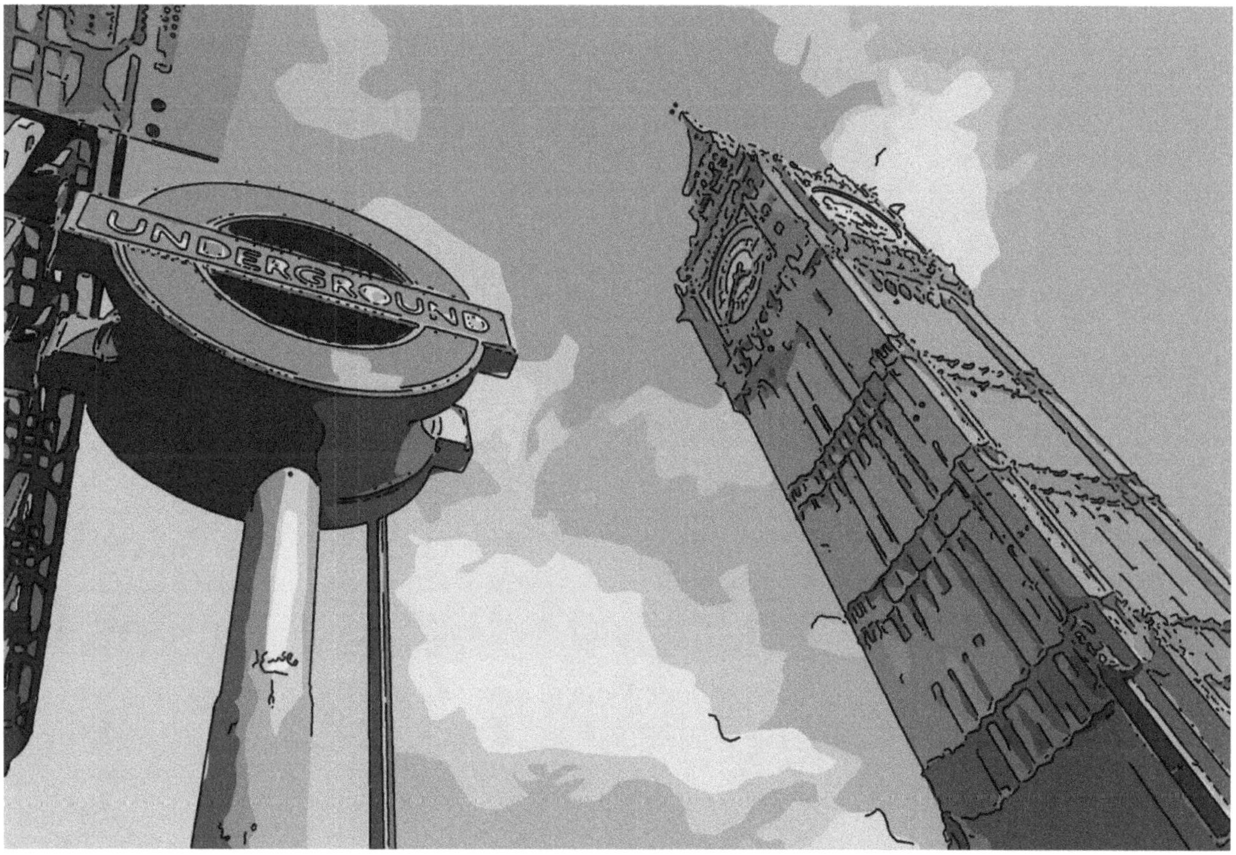

*Annie Jr.*

# London City Sketch
# Adult Coloring Book

Copyright: Published in the United States by Annie Jr.
Published June 2016

ISBN-13: 978-1534779228

ISBN-10: 1534779221

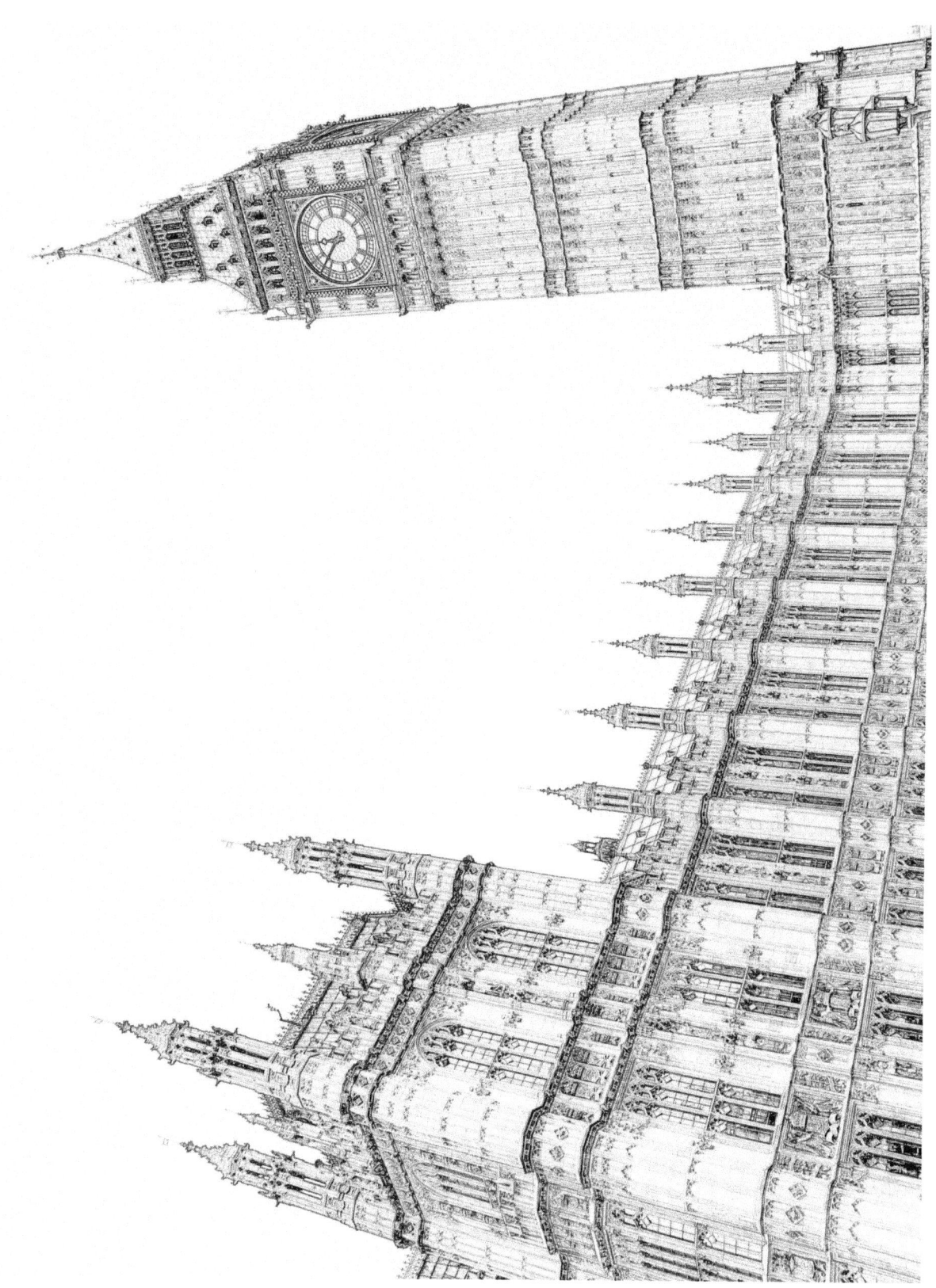

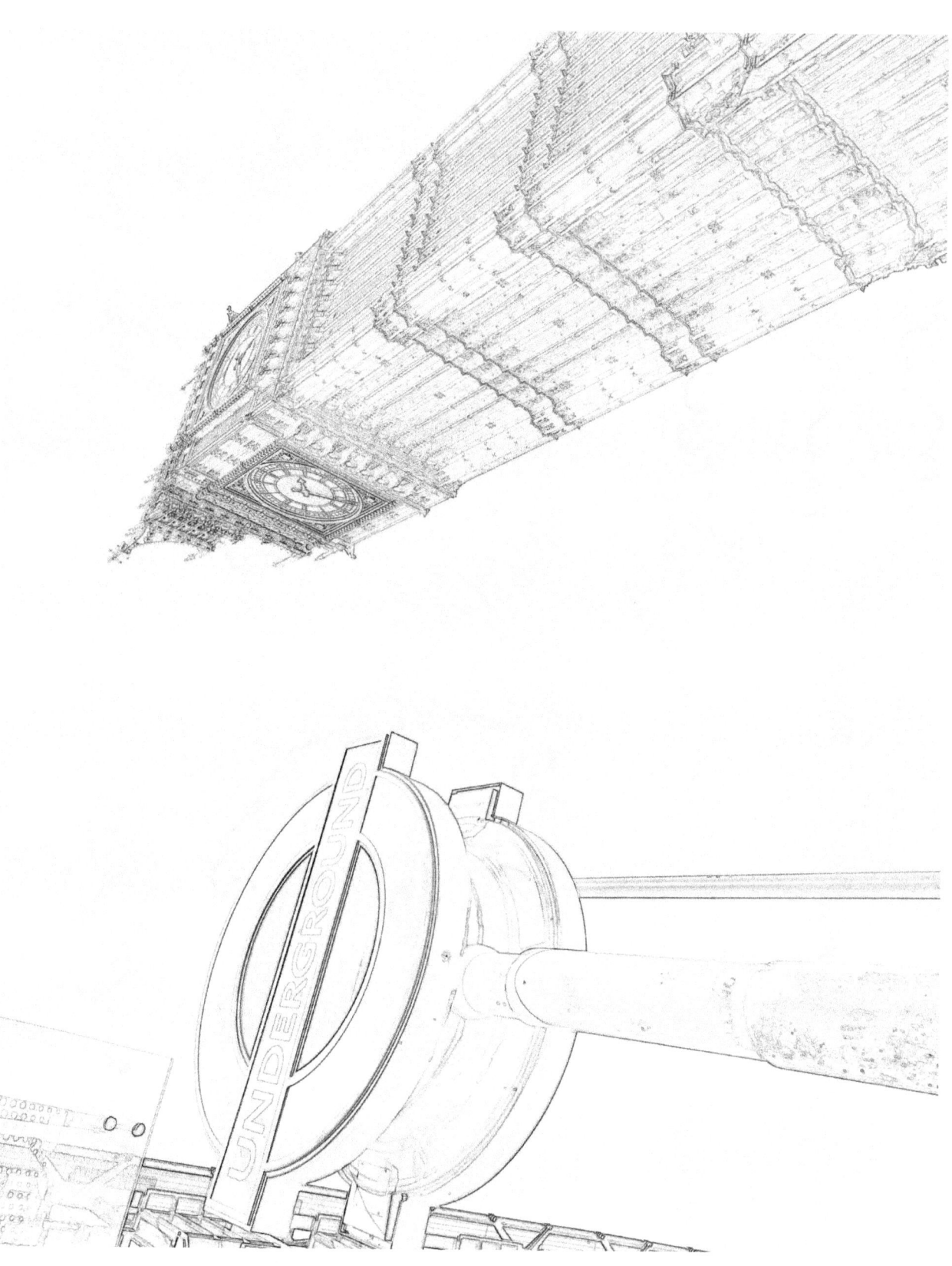

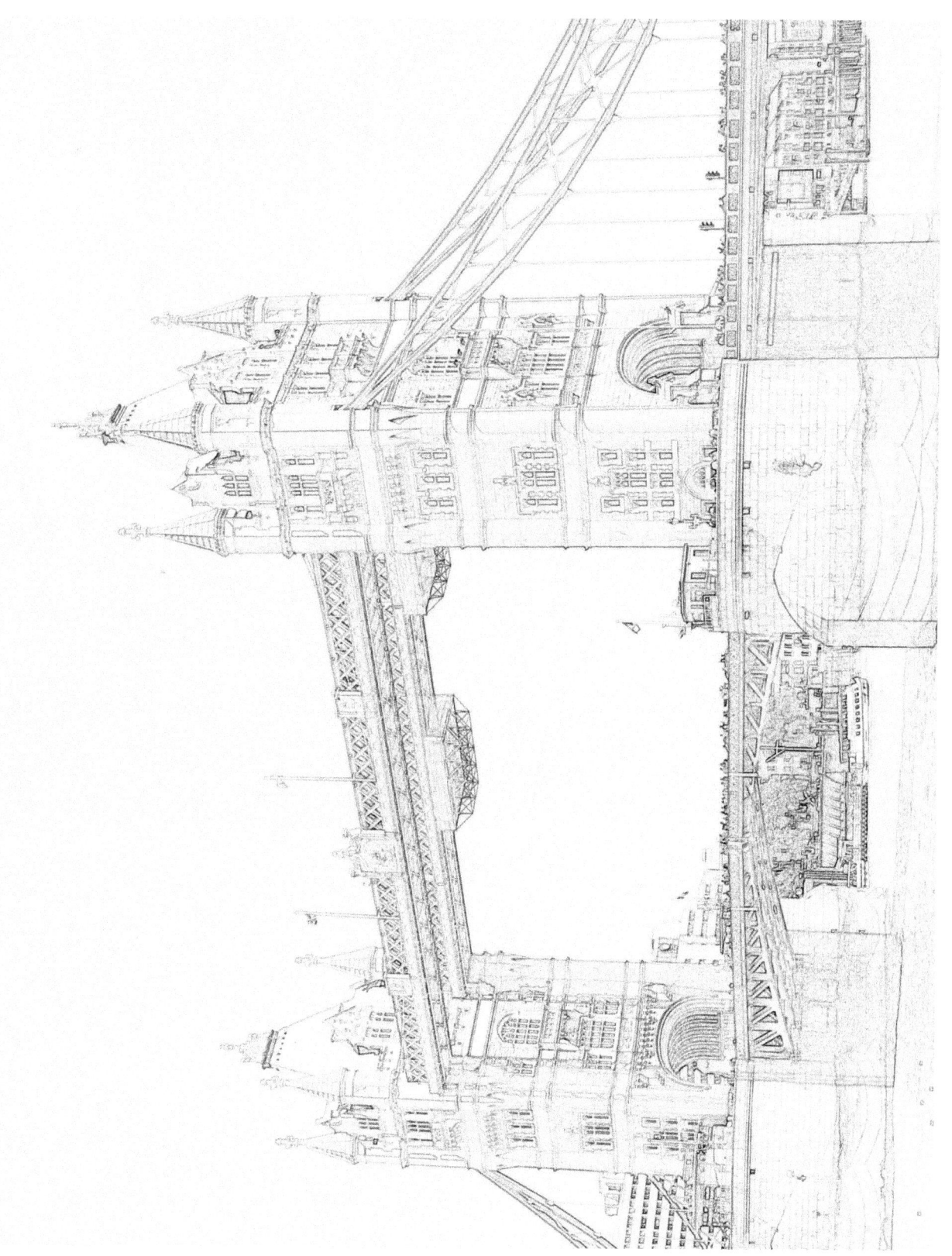

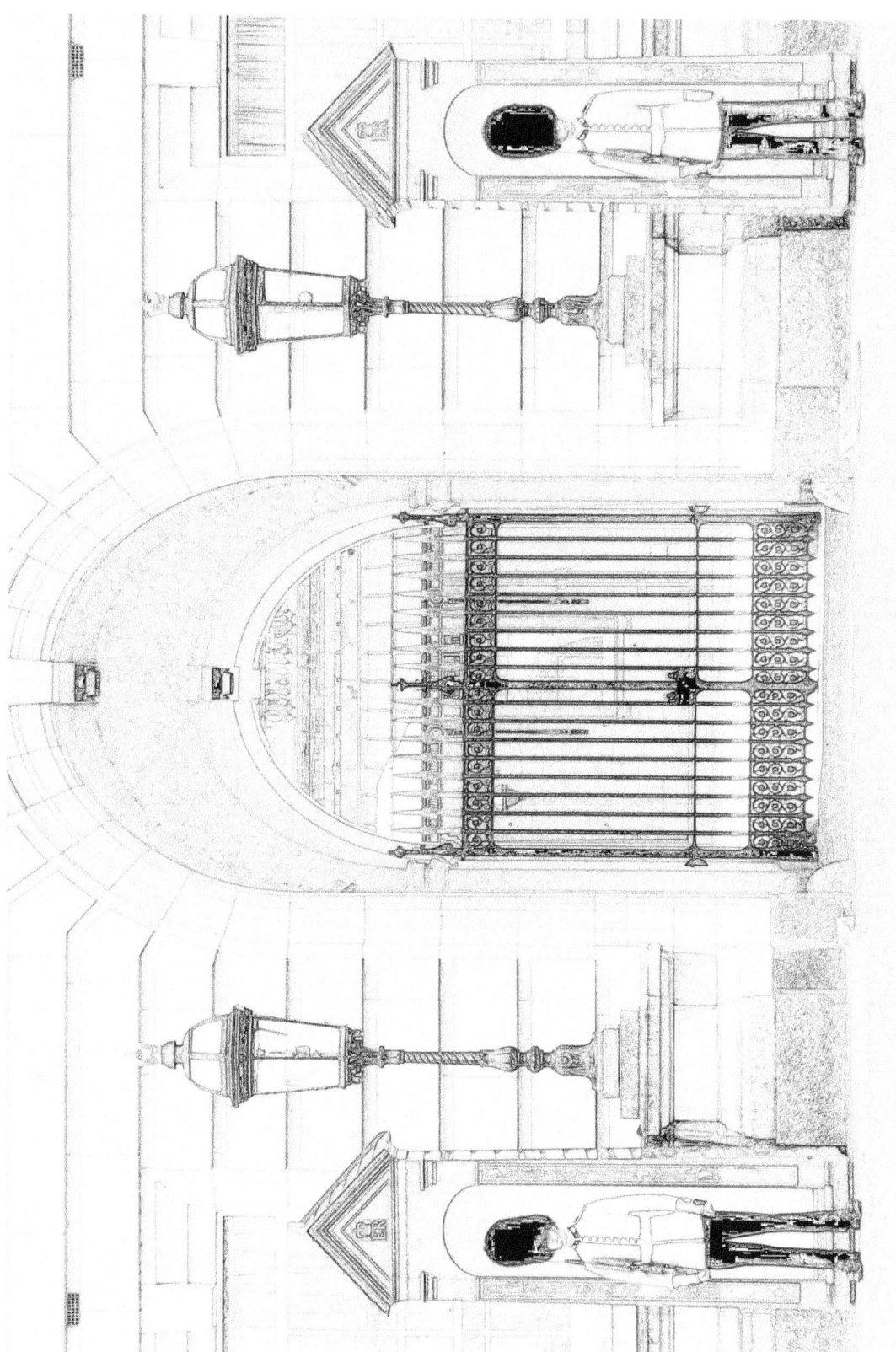

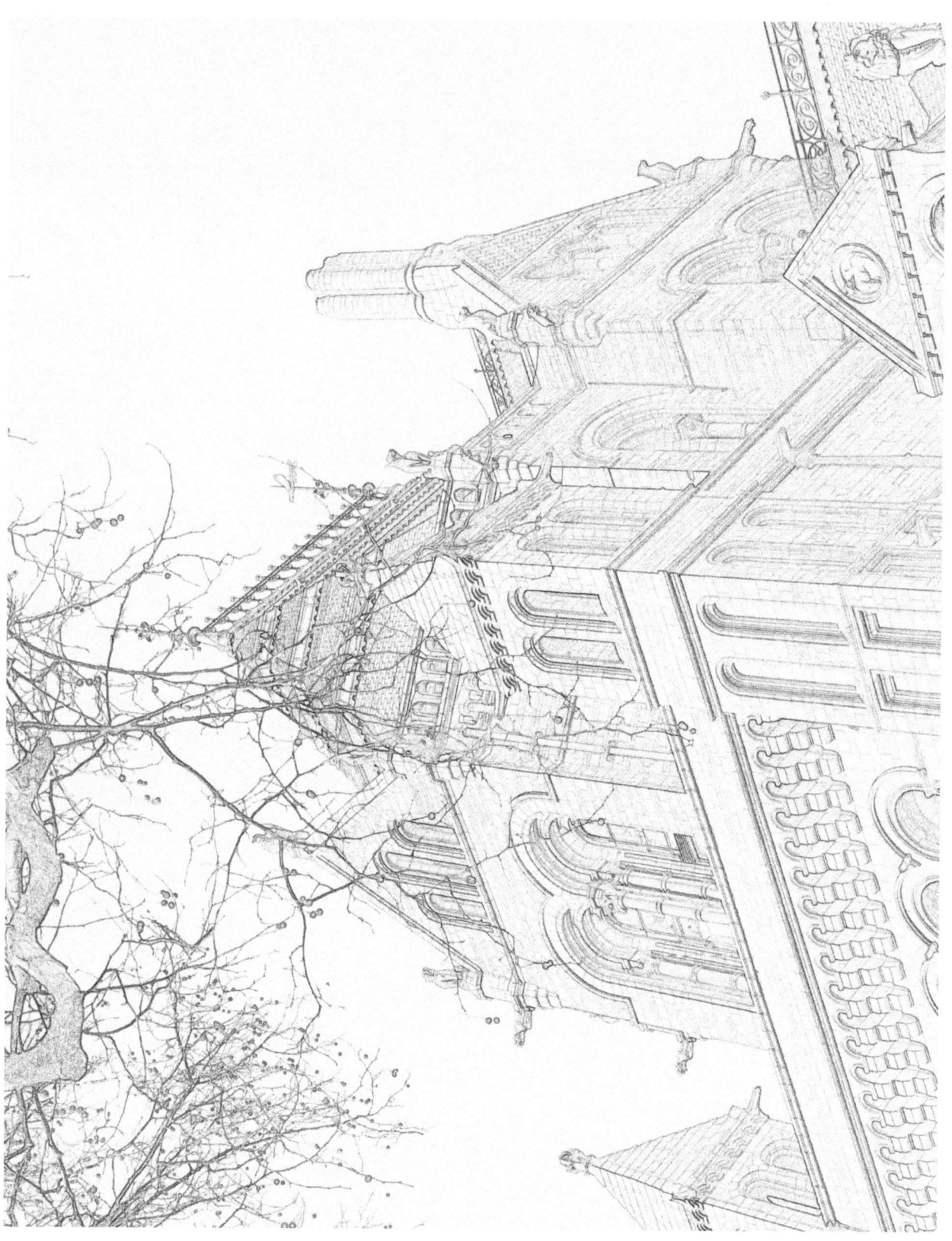

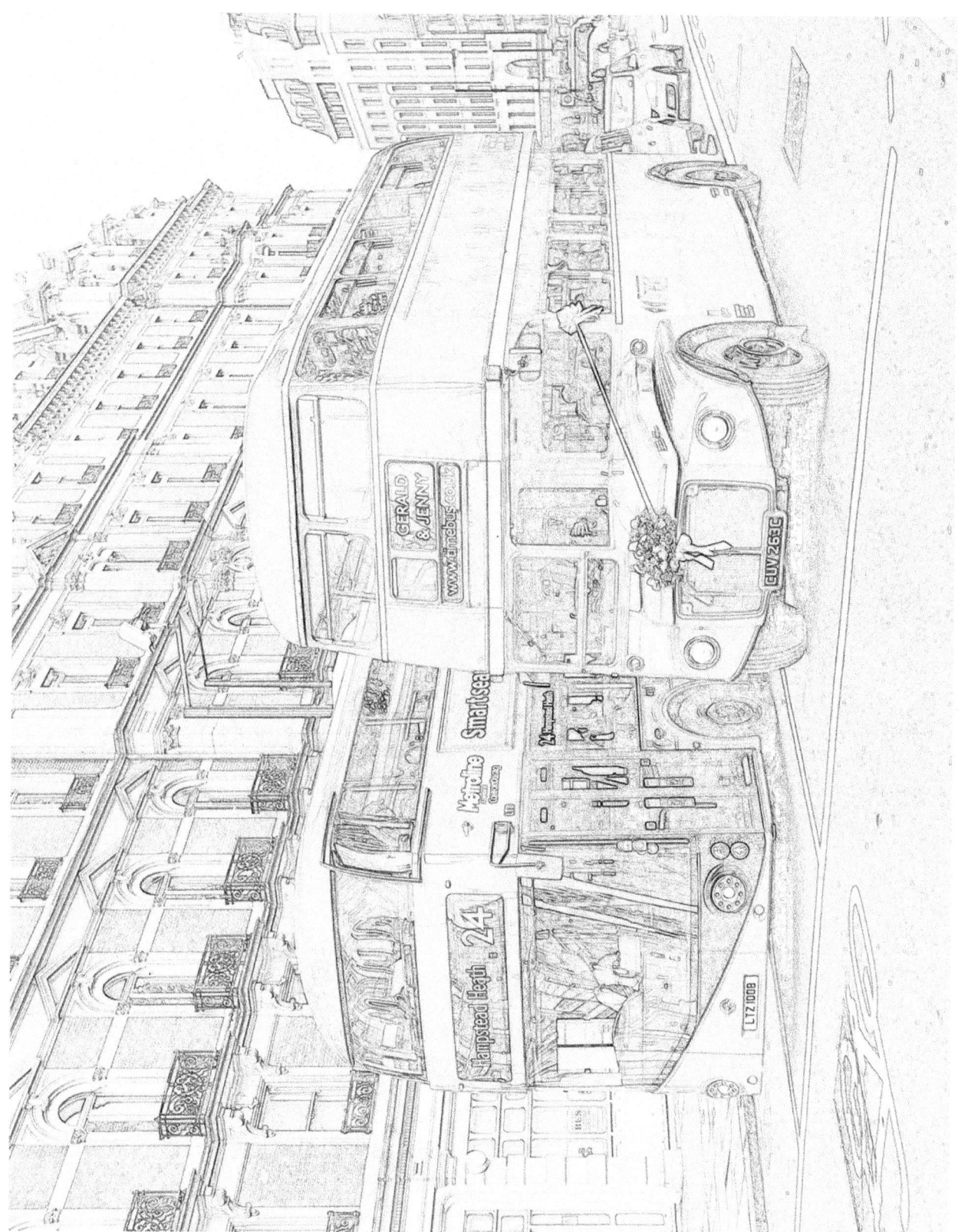

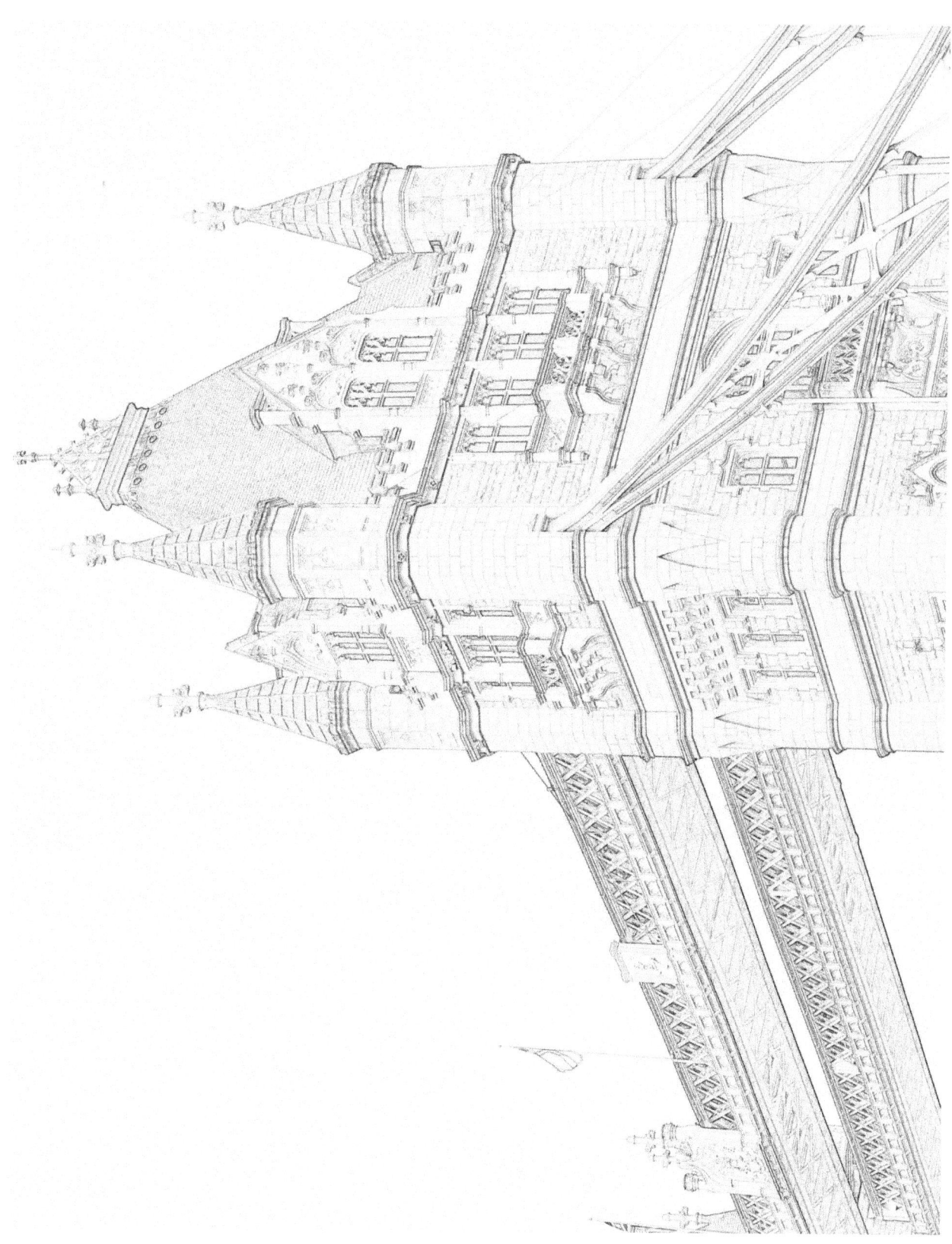

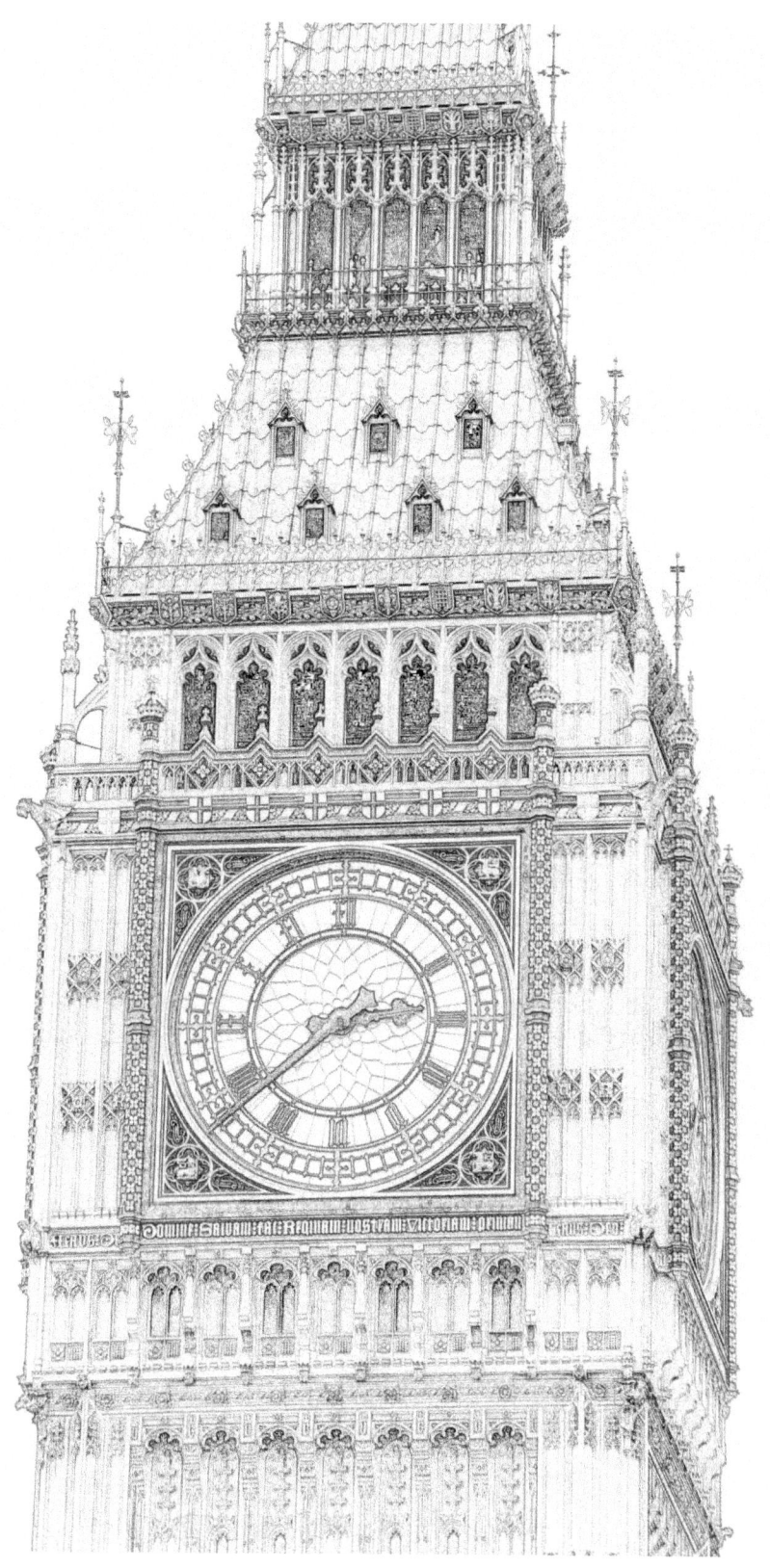

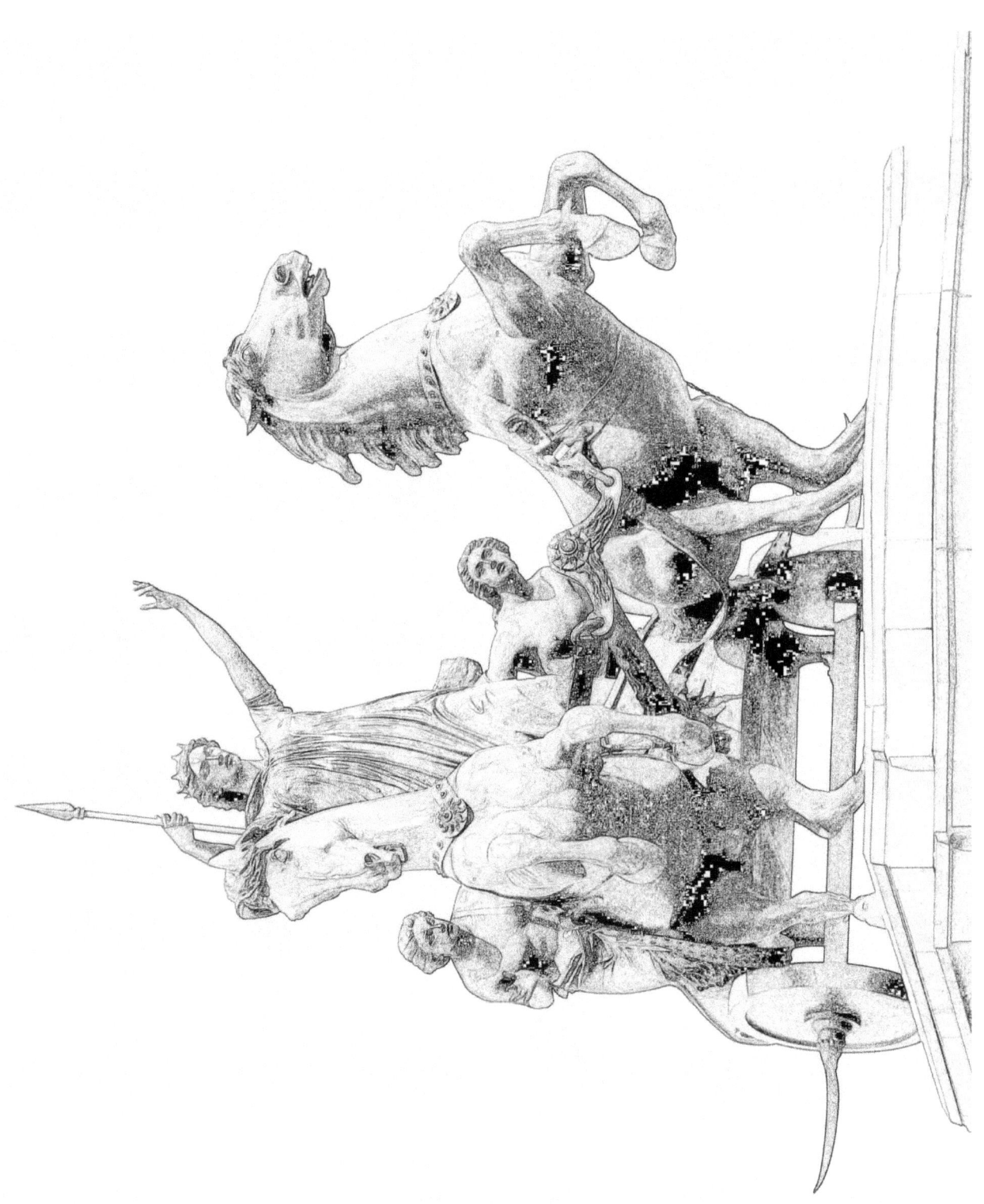

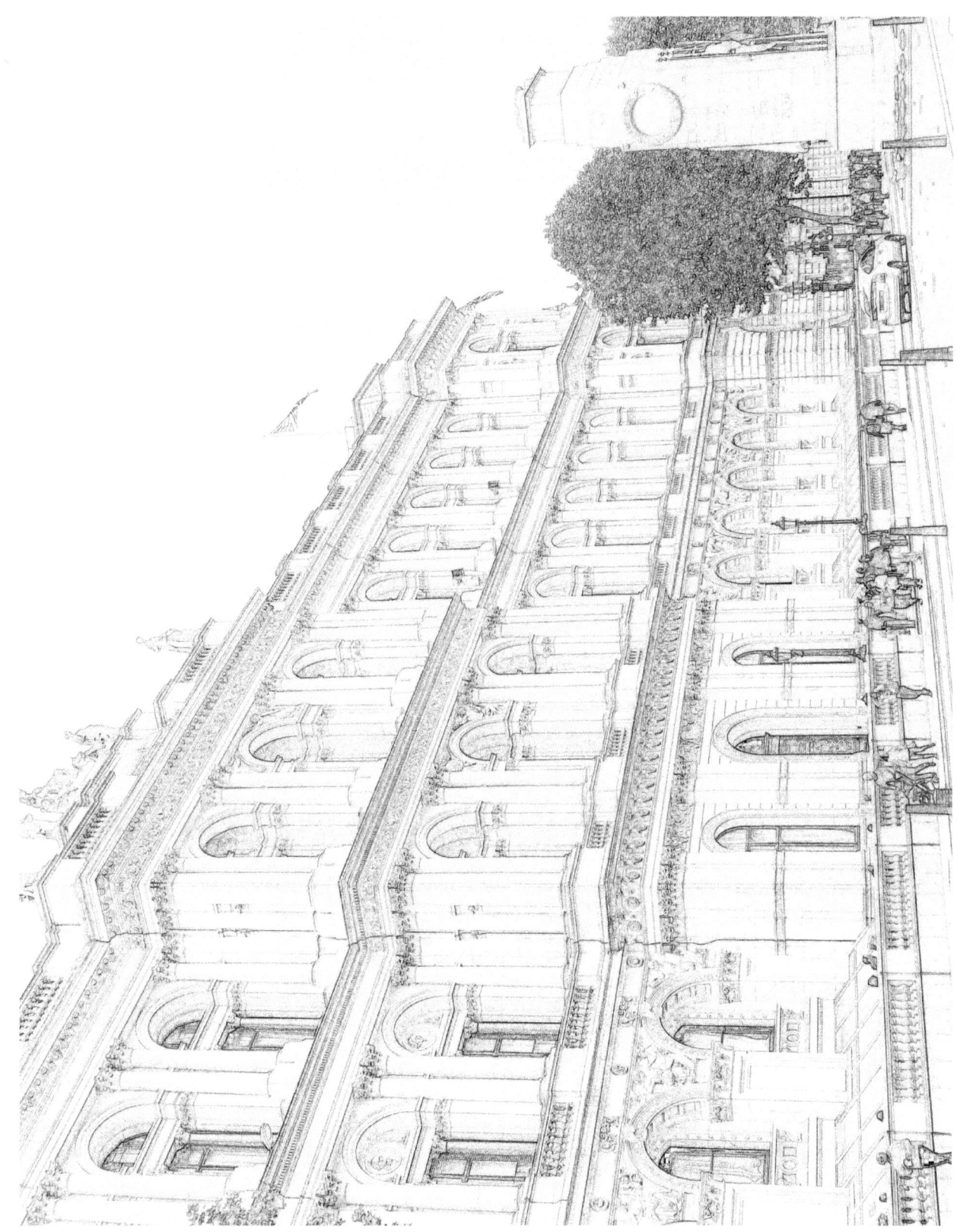

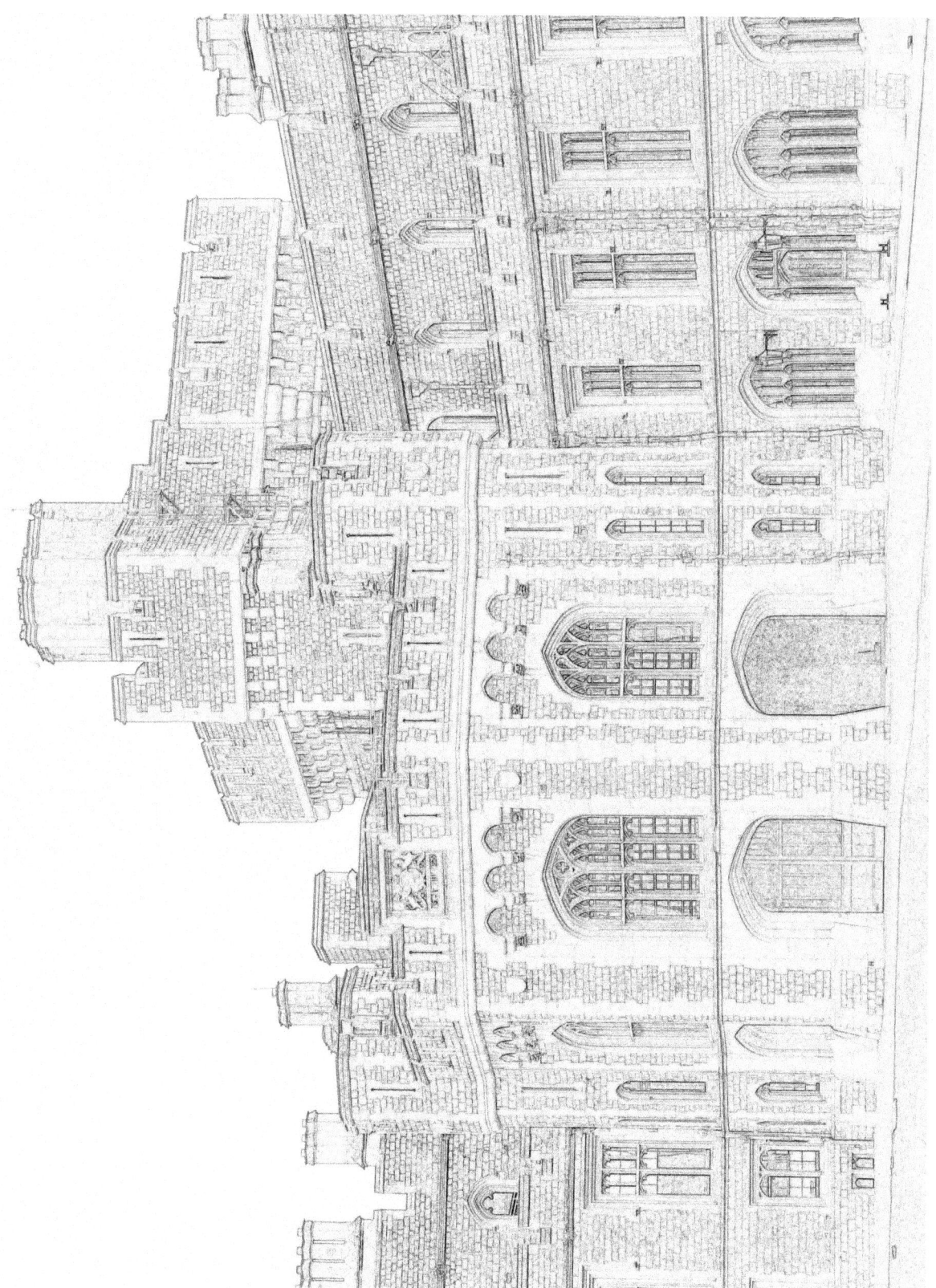

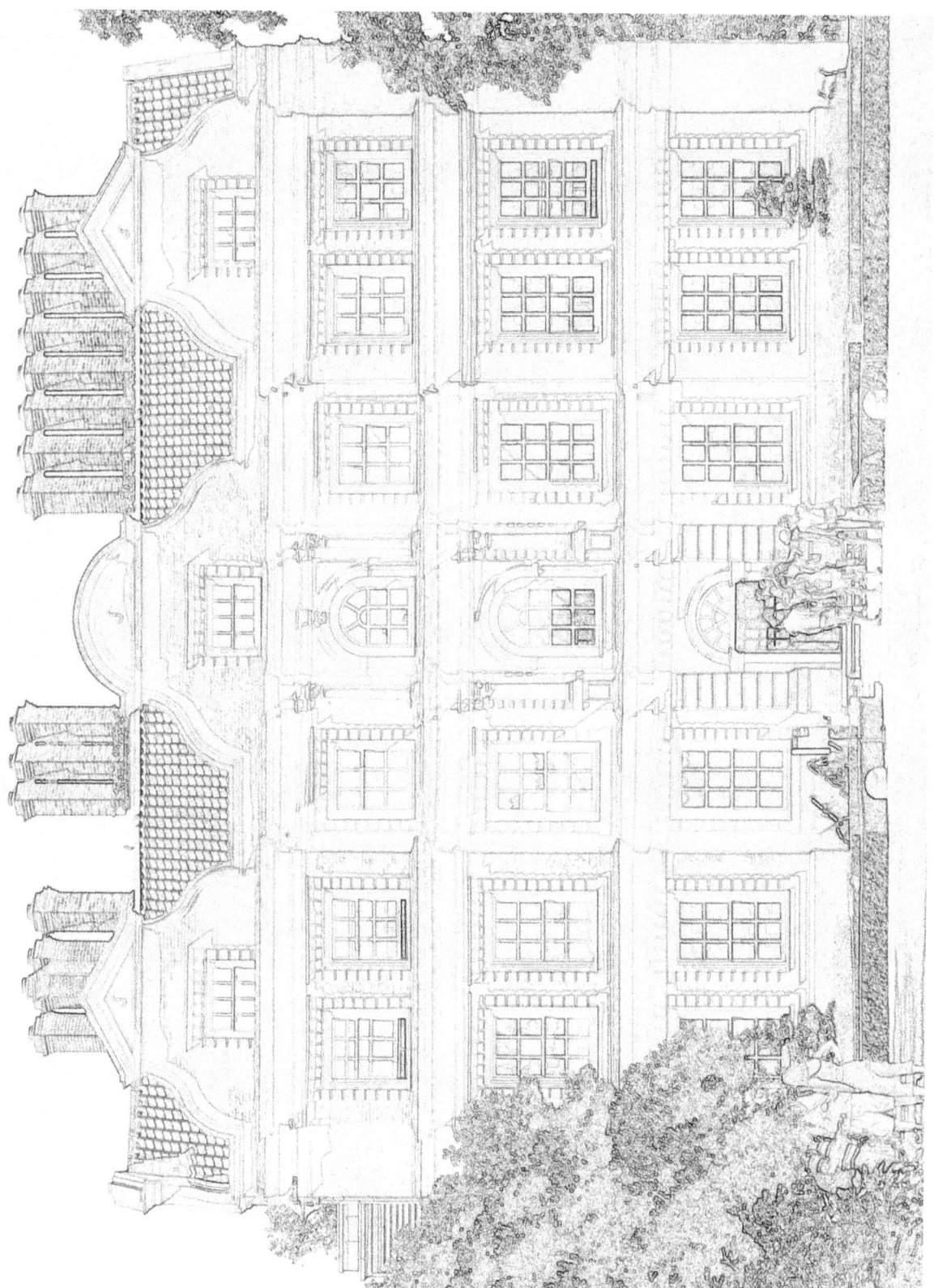

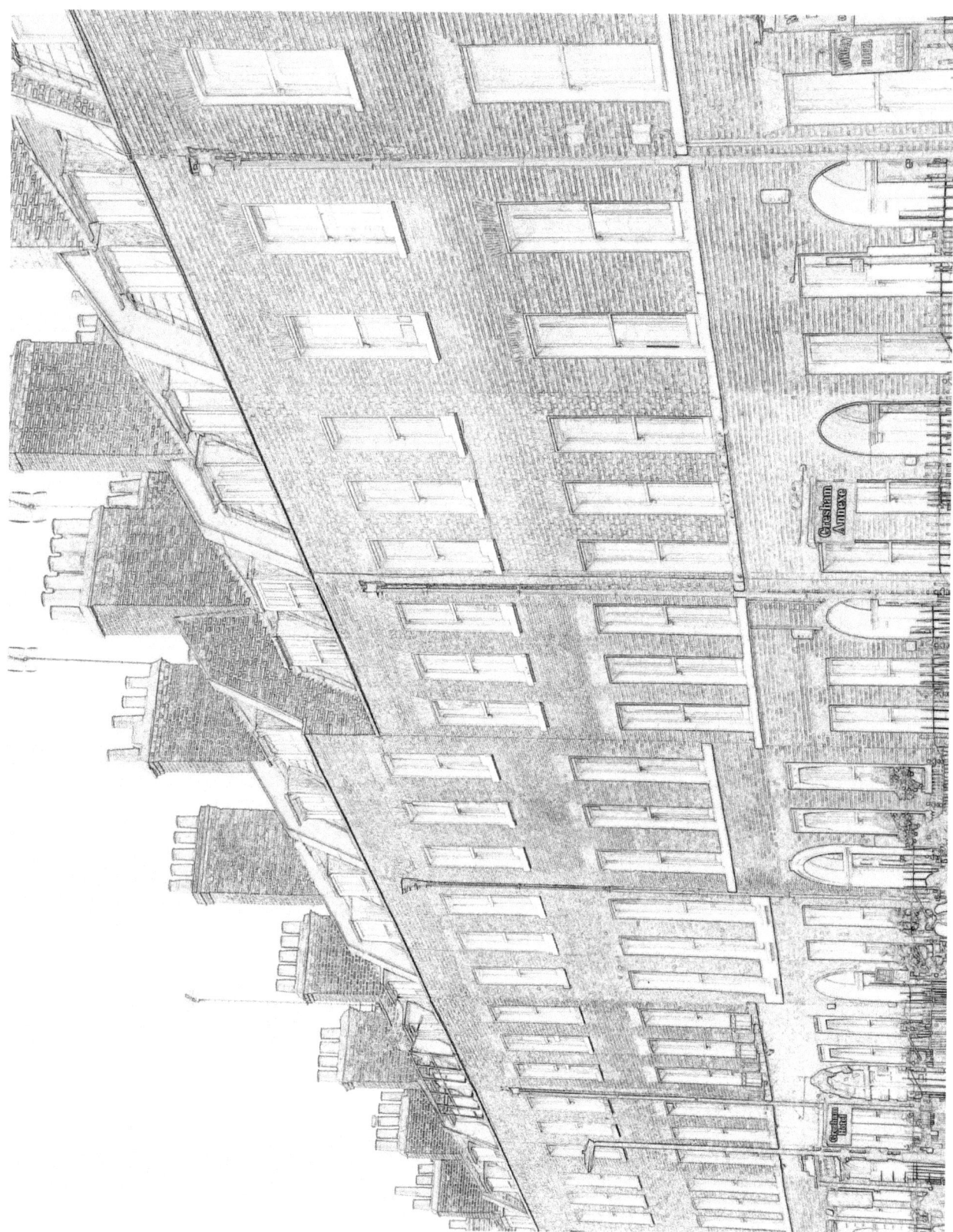

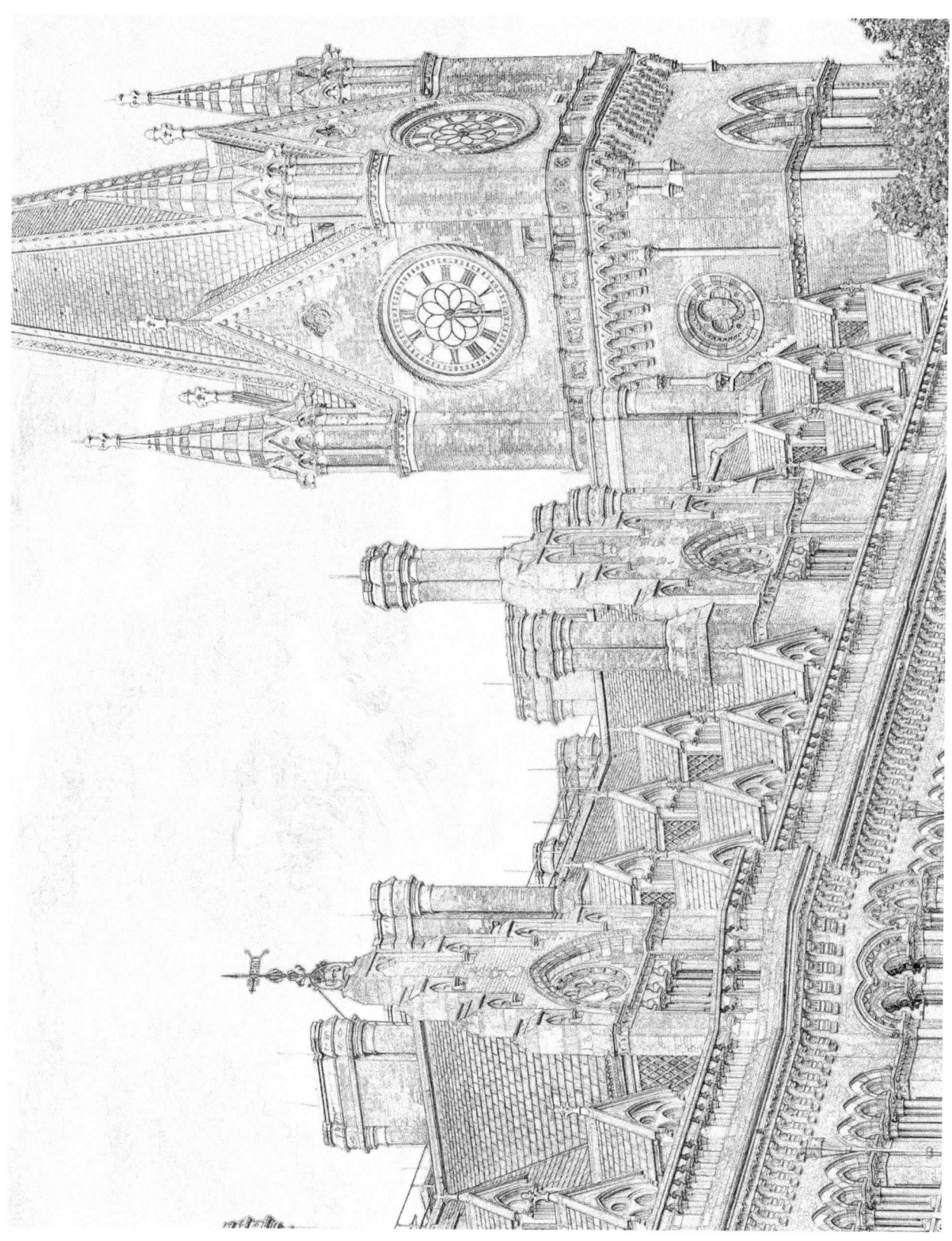

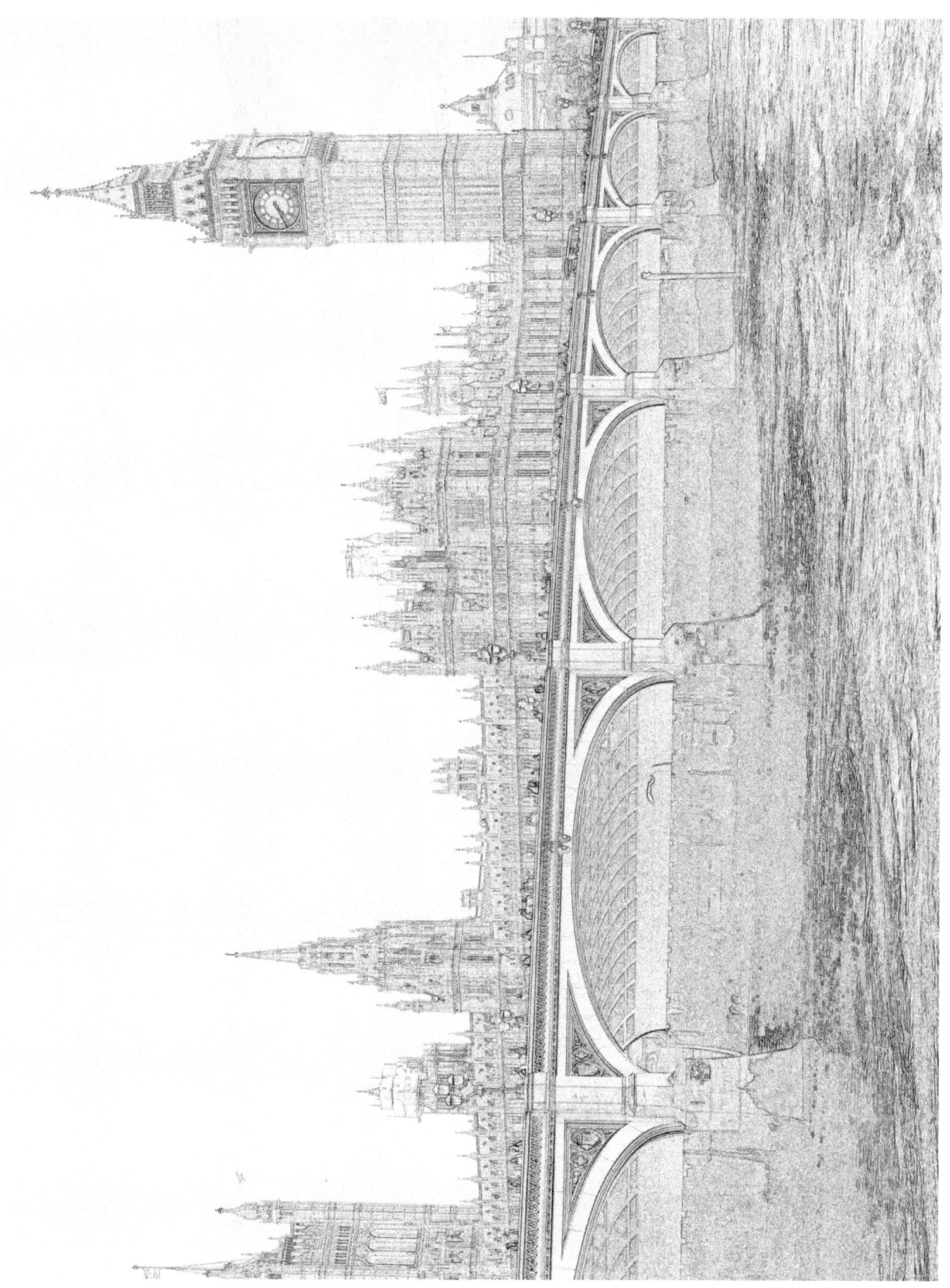

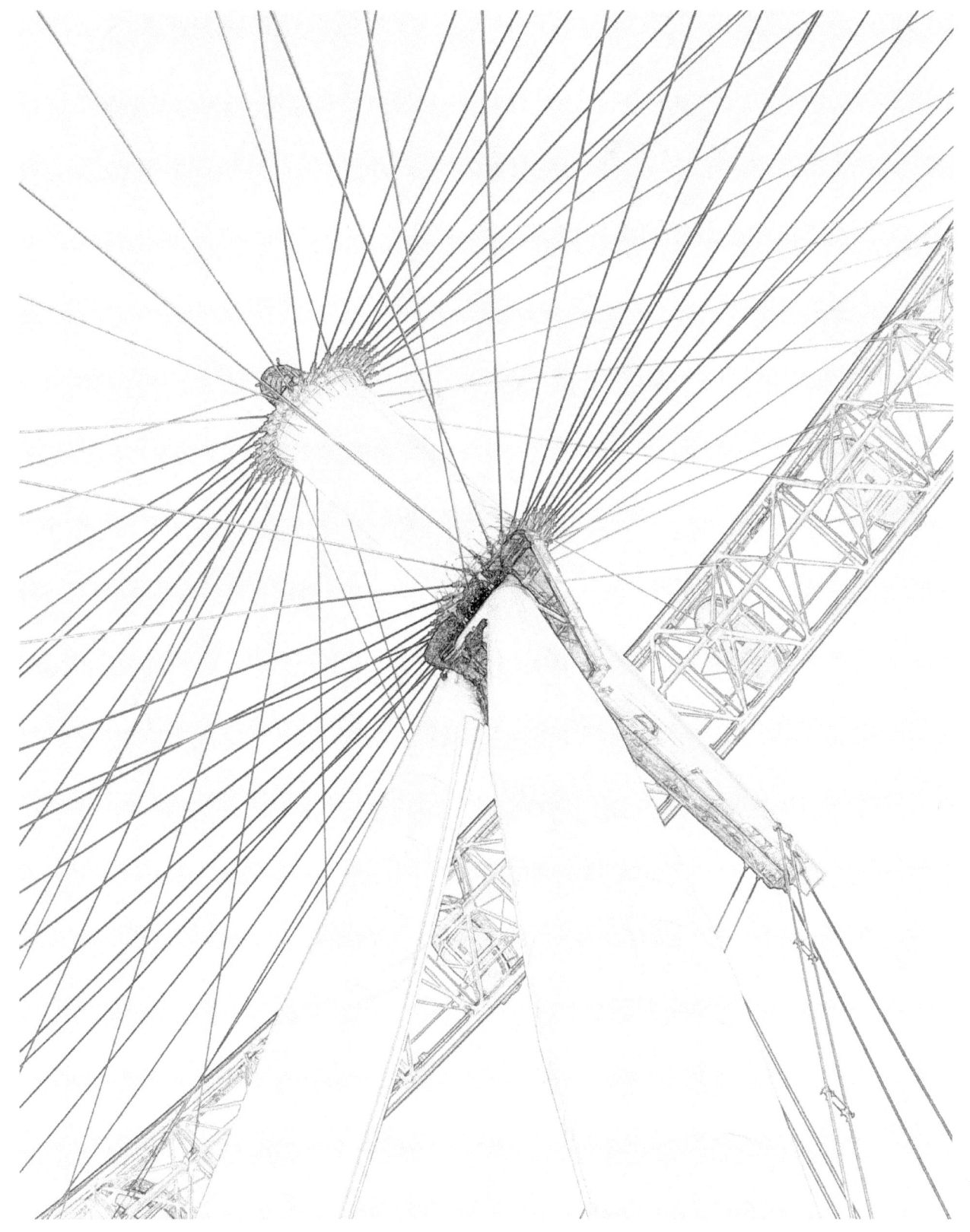

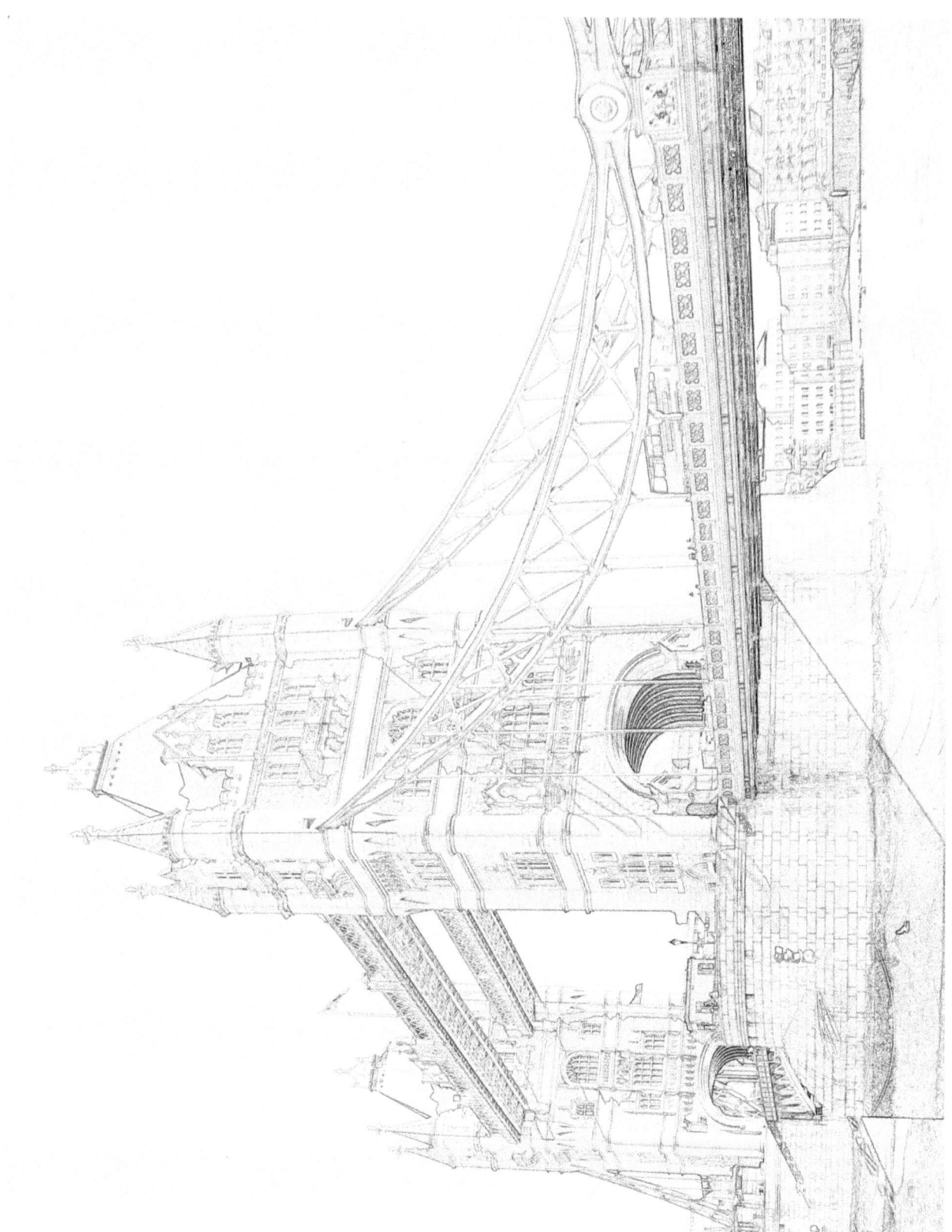

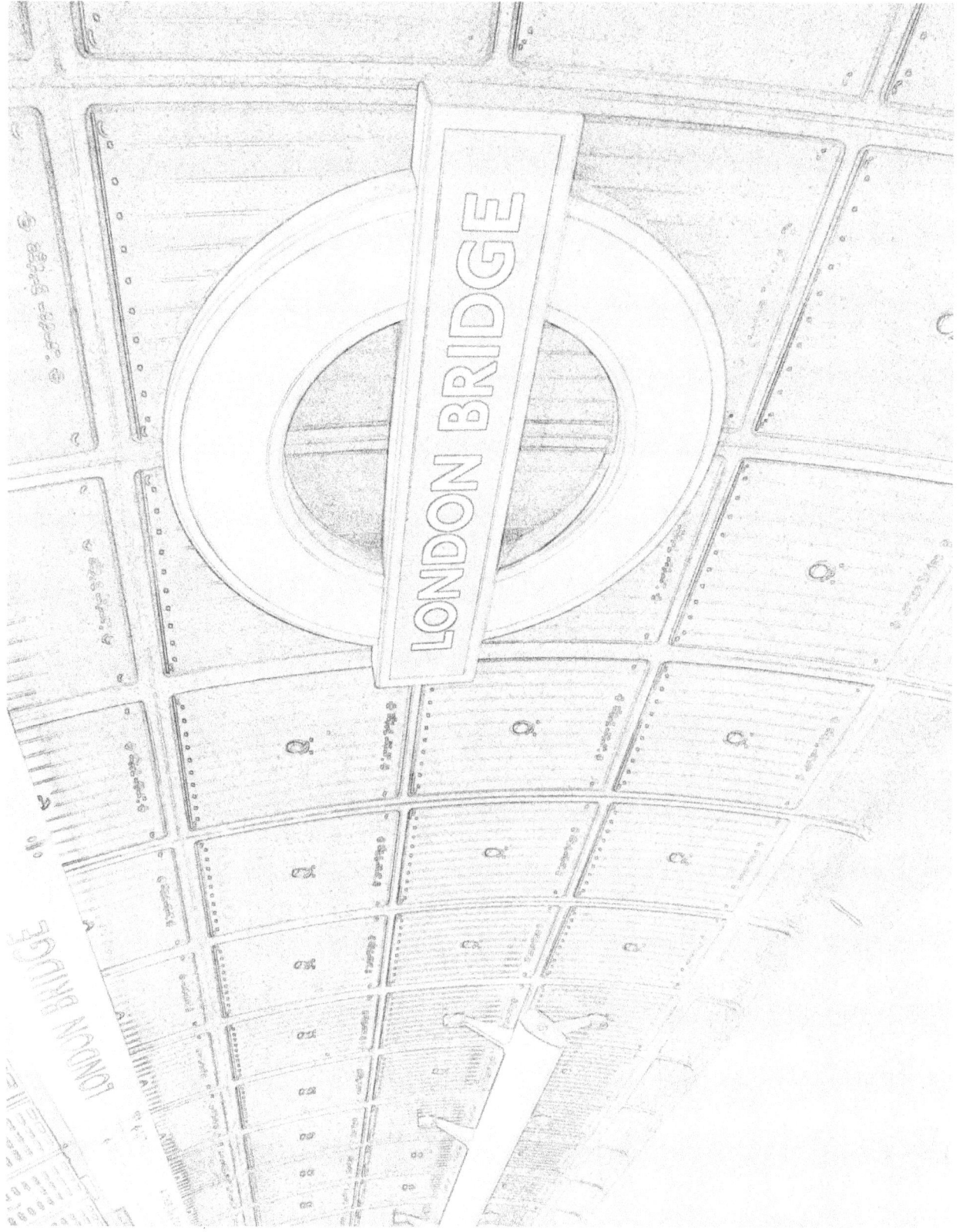

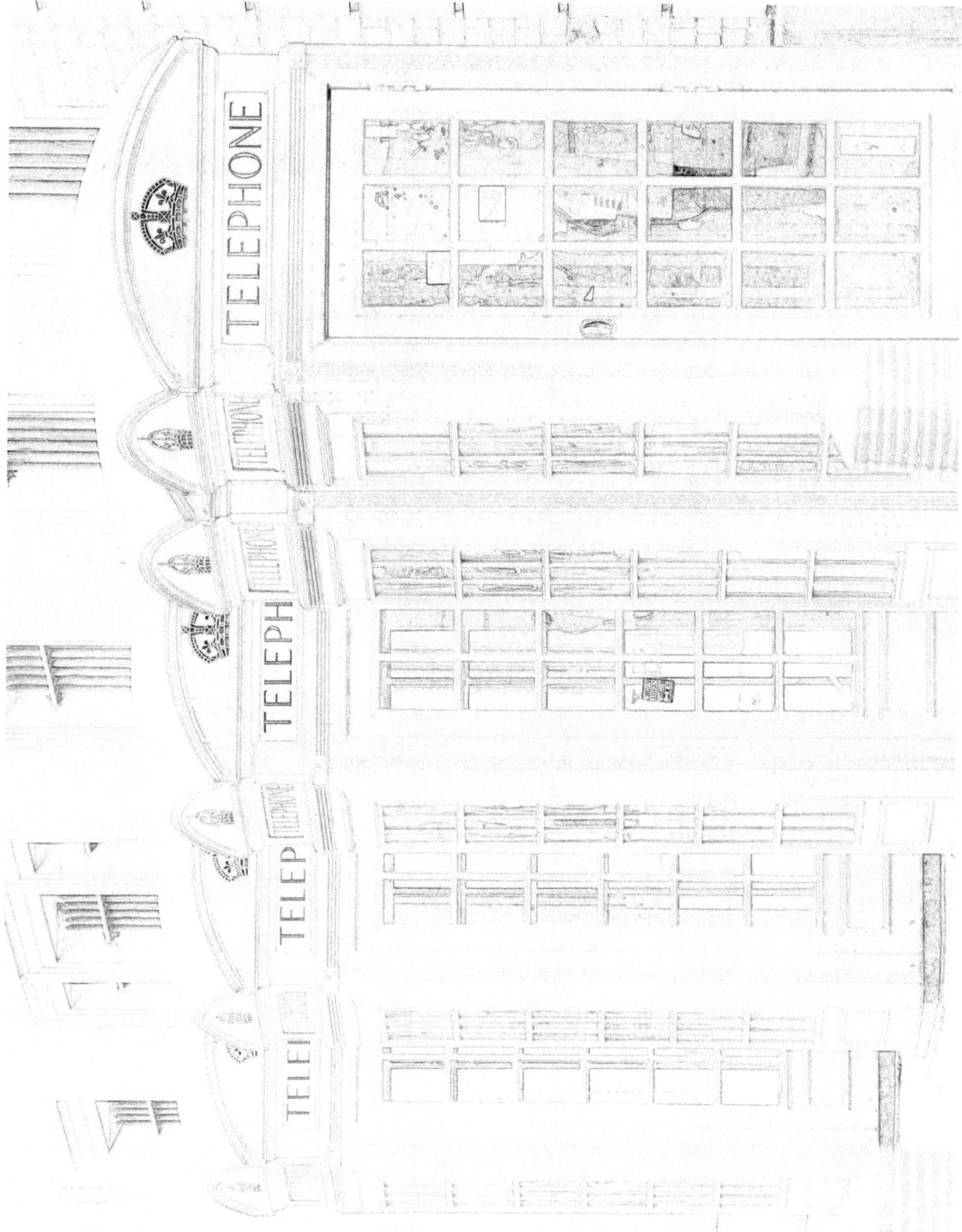

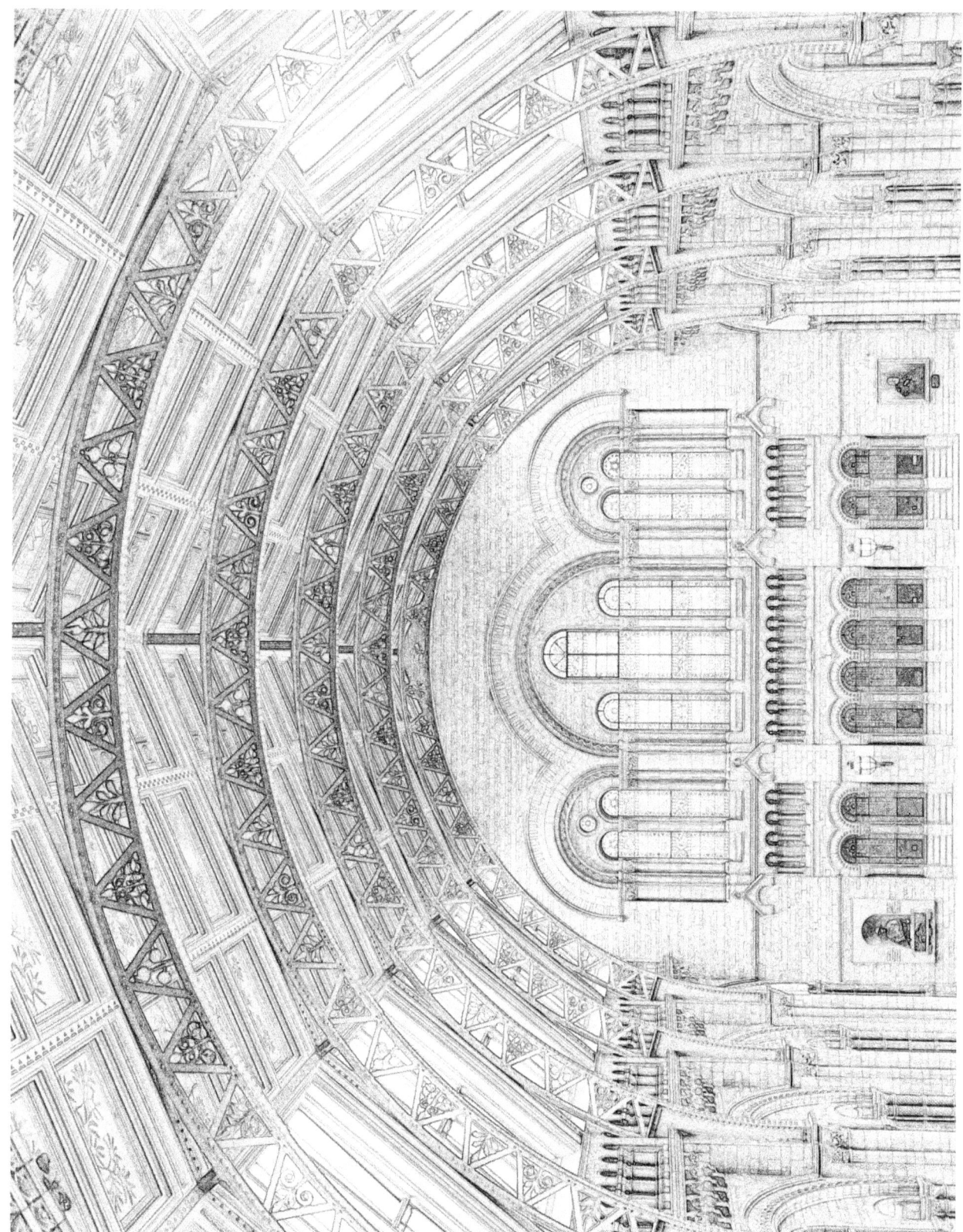

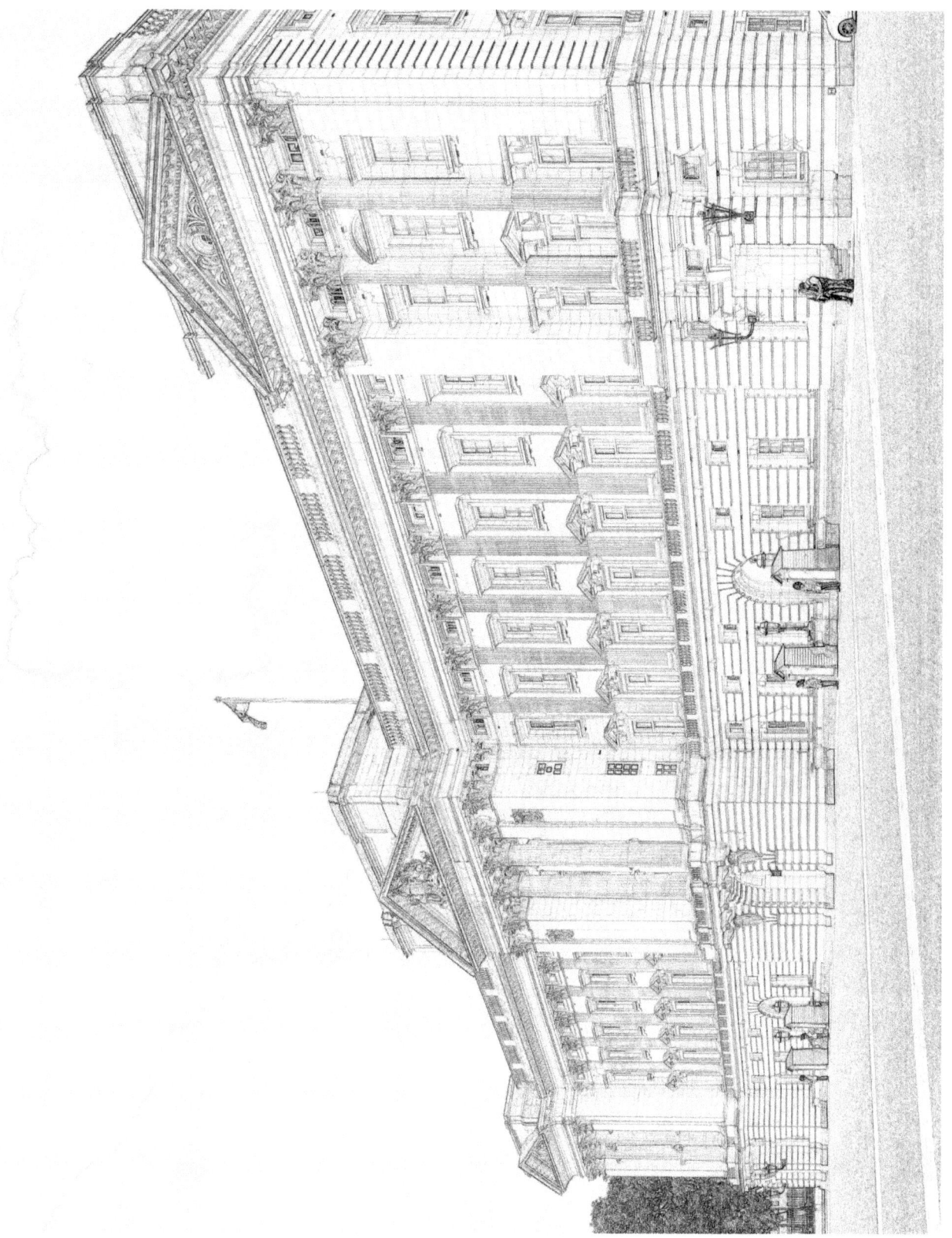

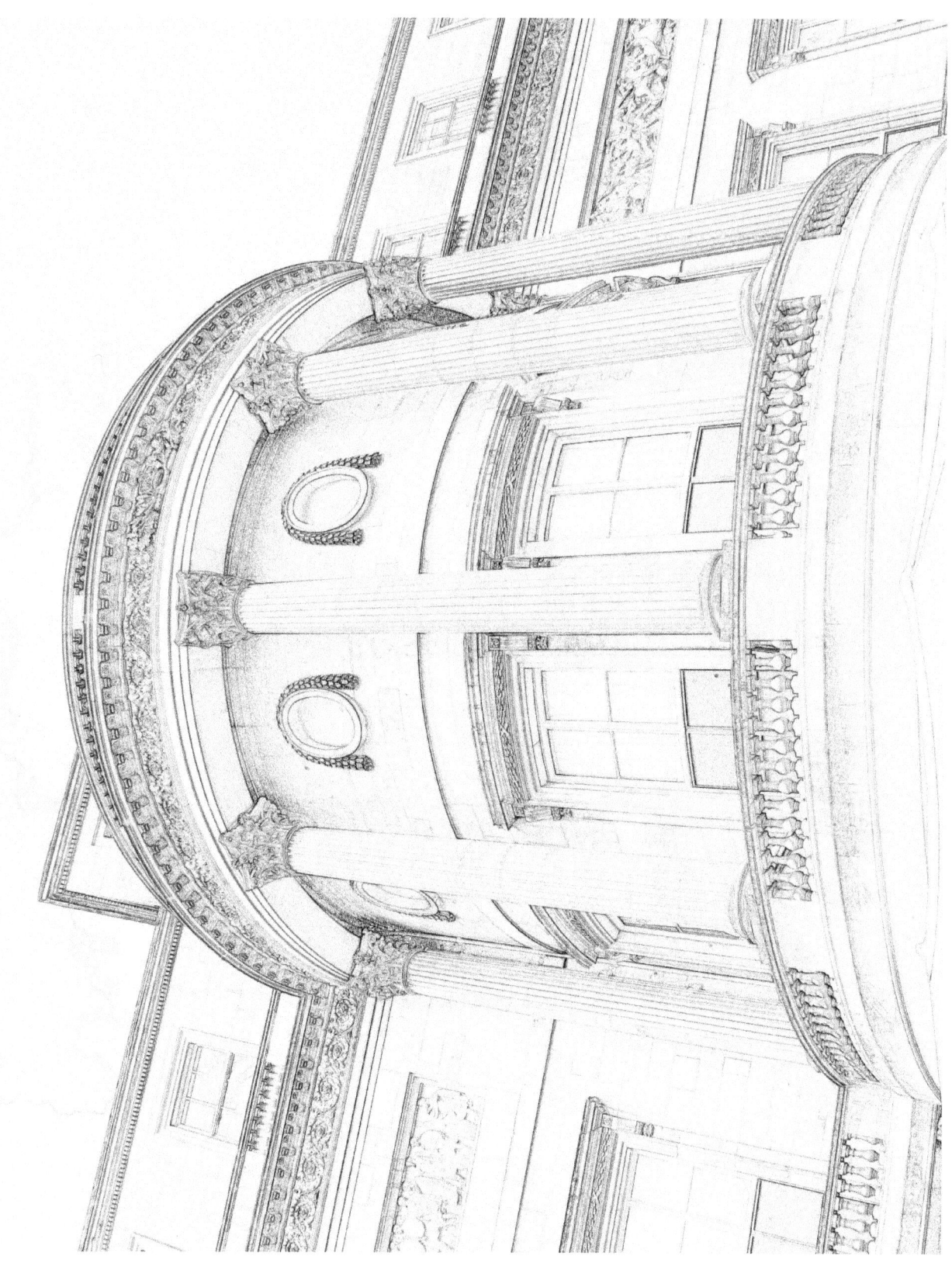

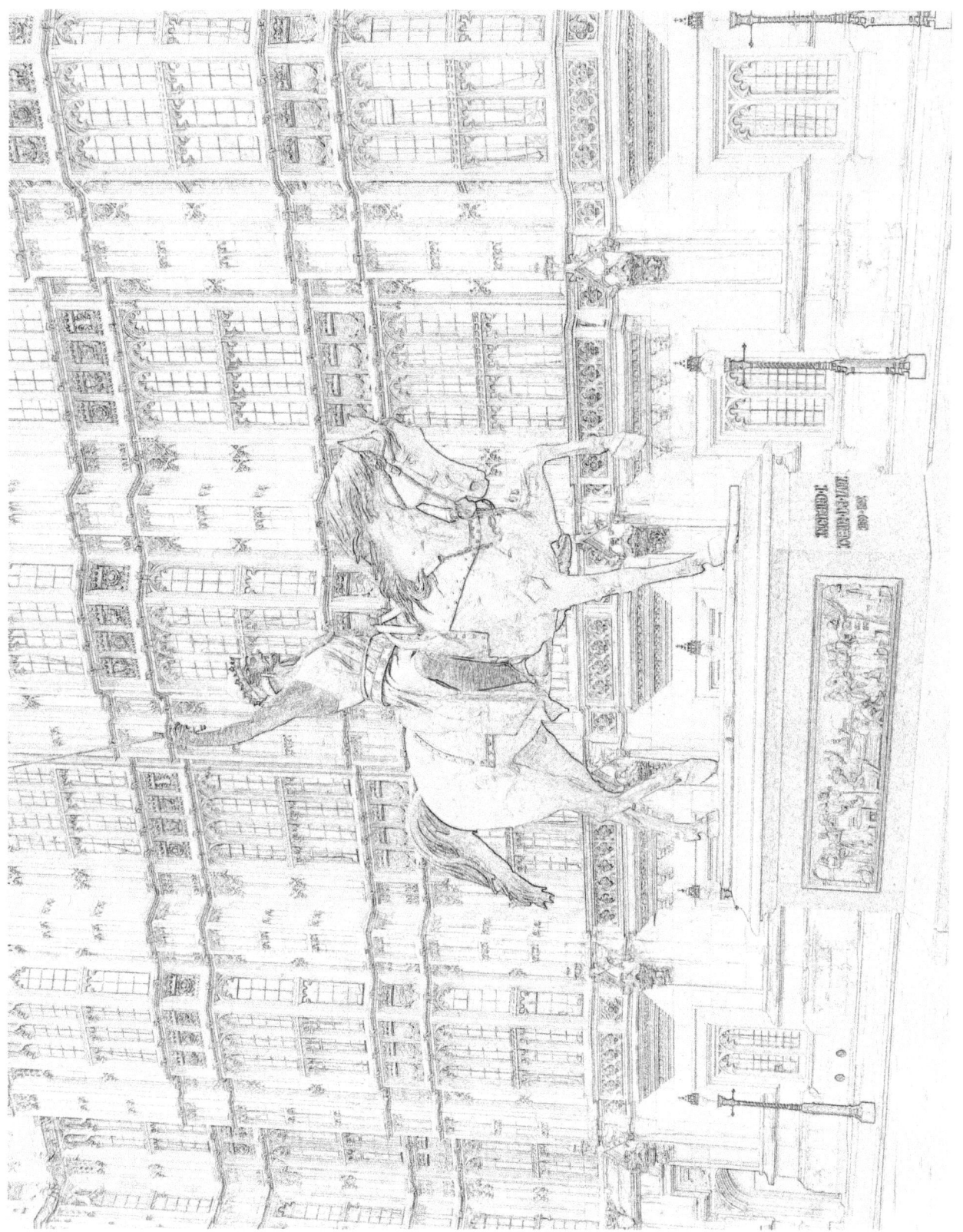

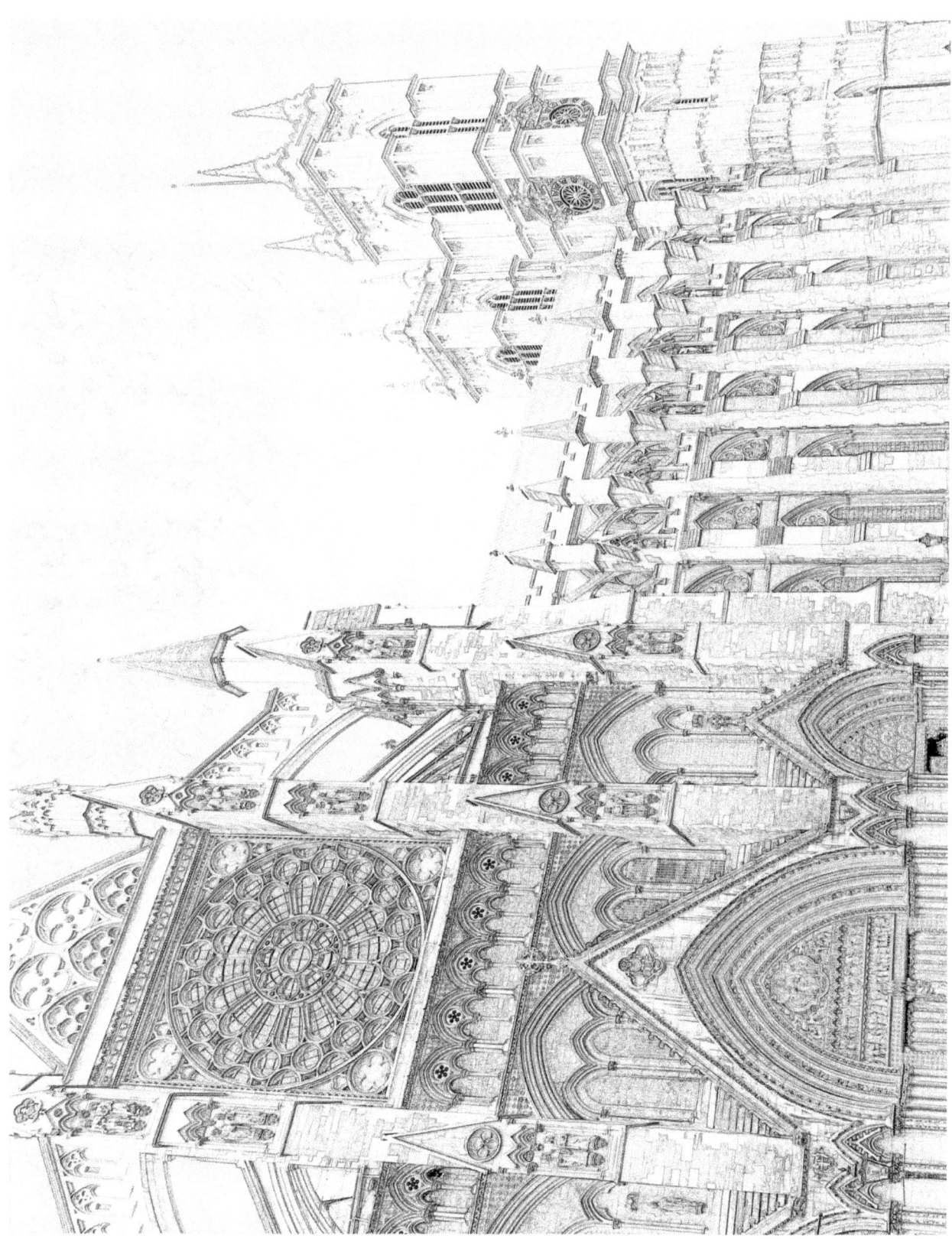

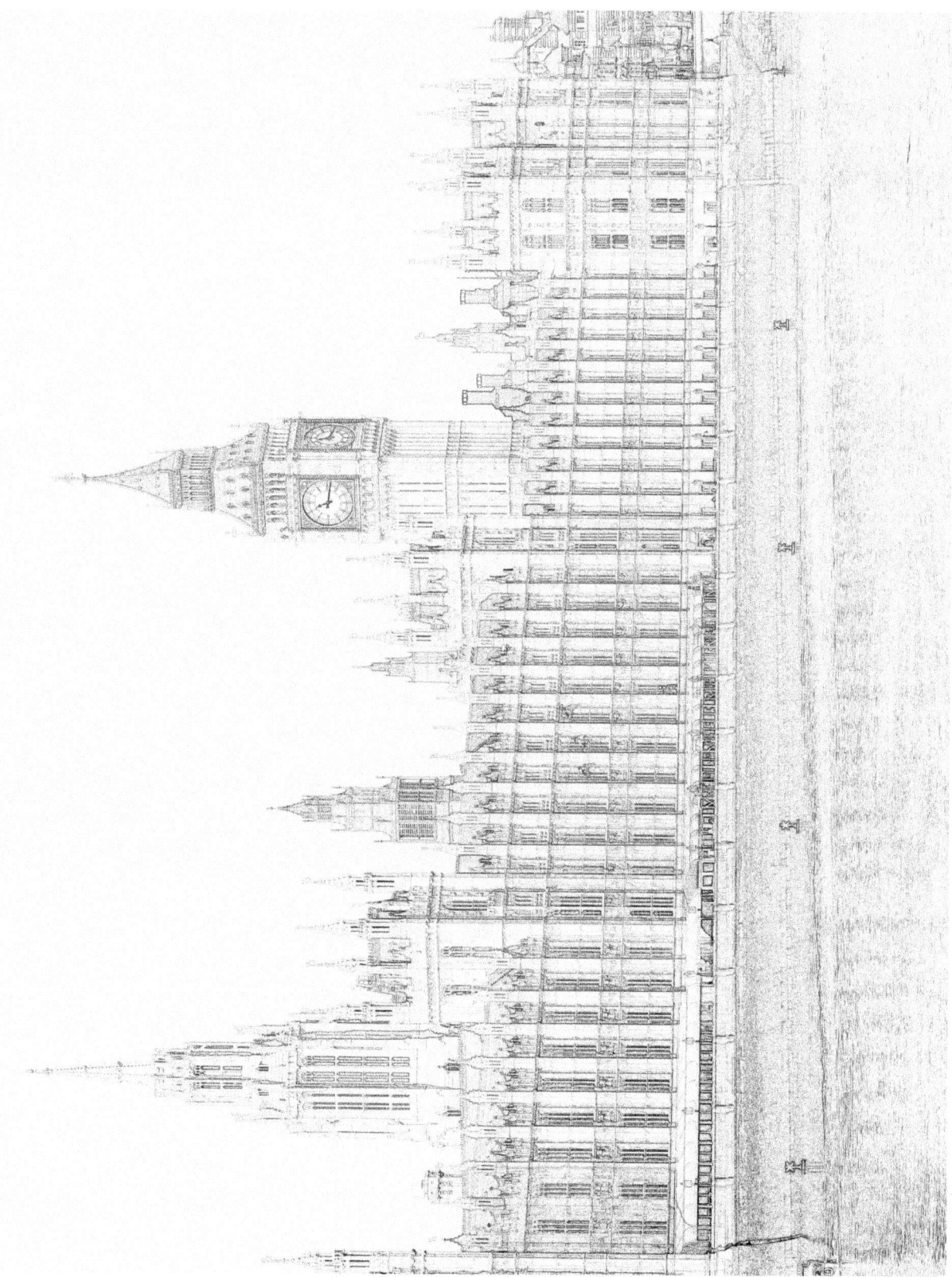

# Thank you

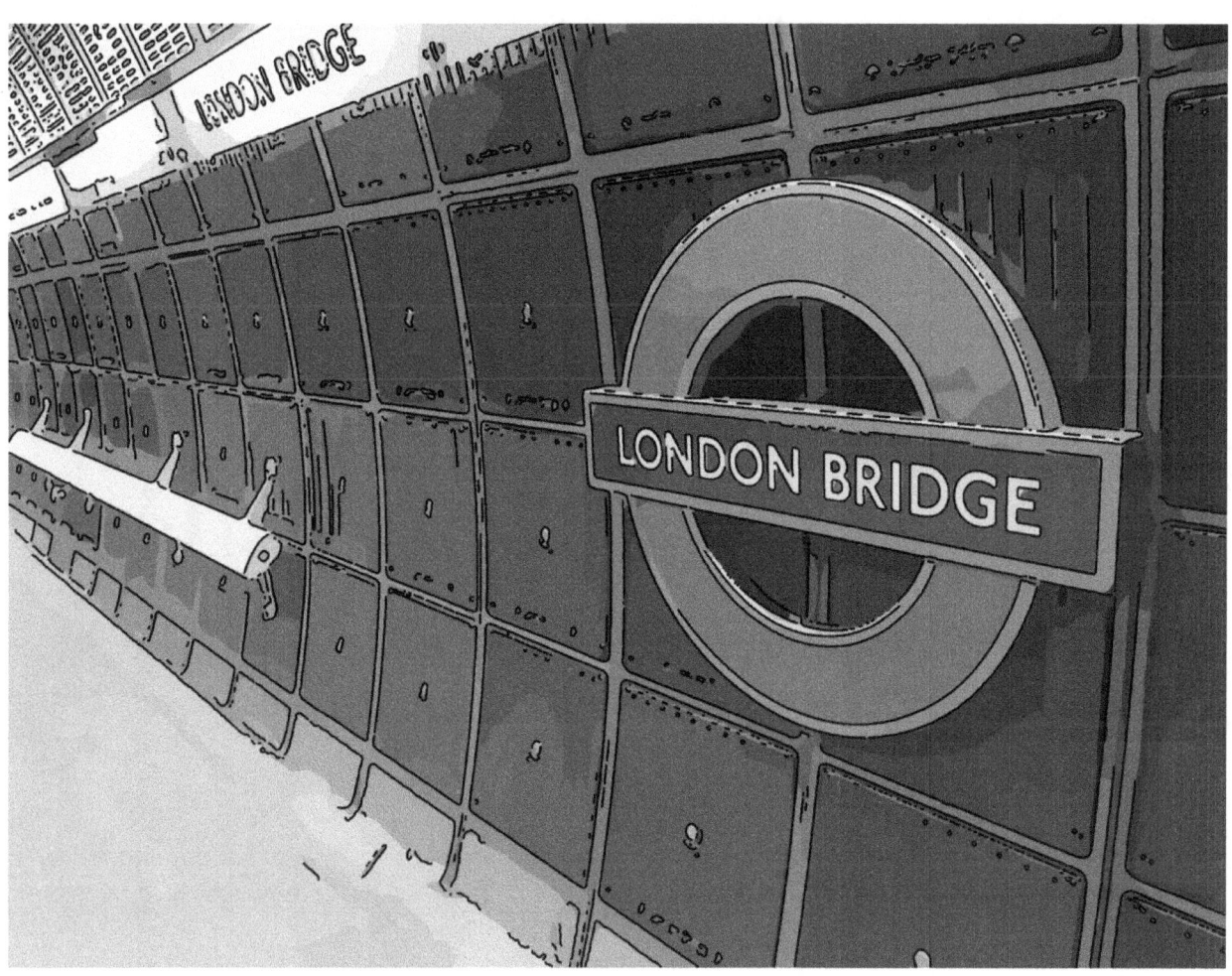